HOW TO GET YOUR PAPER PUBLISHED

Second Edition

By SG Fraser

*This book is dedicated to Alexander H Fraser
that someday he may use it.*

About the author

This book is written by Scott Fraser. He is a practicing doctor in the UK. He has extensive experience of research having written over 100 scientific papers, presentations and books. He is an editor in the Cochrane Collaboration and runs an Evidence Based Medicine Masters degree. He is the editor of six peer reviewed journals and assistant editor of a further four. He is Adjunct Professor at the University of New England, Visiting Professor at the University of Sunderland.

Published in the UK by:-

Anshan Ltd
6 Newlands Road
Tunbridge Wells
Kent. TN4 9AT

Tel: +44 (0) 1892 557767
Fax: +44 (0) 1892 530358

e-mail: info@anshan.co.uk
web site: www.anshan.co.uk

© 2015 Anshan Ltd

ISBN: 978 1 848290 815

British Library Cataloguing in Publication Data

A catalogue record for this book is available from the British Library.

Copy Editor: Andrew White

Cover Design: Scott Fraser

Typeset by: Kerrypress

Printed and bound by: Replika Press Pvt. Ltd.

How to get *your* paper published

Introduction

I will start with a potentially provocative statement – there is no paper that cannot be published somewhere.

Few papers will be accepted for the *New England Journal of Medicine* or *The Lancet*, indeed you should think long and hard before you even consider submitting to these journals. But, generally speaking there IS a place for your paper. If you choose the right journal, conduct the study correctly and ethically and write the paper properly then you will be published. If you miss any of these steps then you won't get your paper published.

You will find as you read this book that certain themes and phrases are repeated a number of times. This is because they are the important determinants of whether you get your paper published or not. They do not represent great insights or scientific secrets to be handed down to forthcoming generations – they are simple pieces of common sense. I know **you** are very sensible but you would be amazed how many of your colleagues send poorly written papers to inappropriate journals and then feel victimized when the paper is rejected.

The three main mantras of this book and the ones you must rigidly adhere to if you want to get your paper published are:

1. Take great pains in writing your paper –attention to detail is everything.

2. Read the instructions for authors and do everything it asks before you submit your paper.

3. Don't give up – bad reviews often contain the advice that makes your paper publishable. Don't get angry- get published.

Stephen King describes writing as telepathy – you are trying to get the reader to see what is in the author's mind. He is writing about fiction of course, but why should medical/scientific writing be any different? Always think of your reader when you write – you understand the work you have done and you want others to have the same understanding – don't let a badly written paper get in the way of this.

This book is written for all those who strive to get their research paper published. Because of my background it mainly contains examples from the biosciences but it is intended to be just as useful for those writing for the social sciences and humanities journals. I am tempted to guarantee publication if you follow the advice of this book, but of course I can't – there are too many other factors over which you will not have control and so you do need some luck. However the ethos of this book reflects that of Louis Pasteur - *'Fortune favors the prepared mind.'*

The aim is to make this book both accessible and comprehensive. If you feel either of these needs is unmet please email with your suggestions for improvements.

Contents

Section 1. Ten ways to make sure your paper is published

For those who are desperate to rush ahead and don't want the tiresome business of having to read a whole book, here are the Ten Top Tips for getting your paper published. If you want more tips and more detail (attention to detail is one of the most important tips) and therefore to increase your chances of being published, then read the whole book.

1. *Think* – do I really need or want to publish a paper? If the answer is no then stop. Is the cinema open? Are your friends and family free? There are **lots** of better ways to spend your time.

2. Have you anything to say? It is not a problem to publish an interesting case that is already described in the literature, but do make sure you have something to add – even if it's your own views.

3. If you do feel you have something to say, what type of paper are you going to say it with? You don't need to embark on a randomized controlled trial or a giant population based study (it's unlikely you will get the money anyway) to get published. Case series, case reports, reviews, letters to the editor are all perfectly valid.

4. What sort of journal are you aiming to get into? If you need a high impact factor journal to get your next grant then this matters. If you simply want to get your name 'out there' you will have to be more modest in your selection of journal.

Make sure the subject of your article is the type they accept in the journal you are aiming for.

5. Plan and execute your study correctly and ethically. If you don't it will be obvious to the peer reviewers.

6. Take great pains when writing your paper. Stick closely to the guidelines for authors for the journal you have chosen. Take great care structuring the paper as the journal wishes, with grammar, style and spelling. These really DO matter.

7. Write the paper so someone can read it. It is not a short story but it needs a beginning, middle and an end. The reader wants to know why you did something, how you did it and what you found. The more readable the paper is the more likely it will be accepted by a journal.

8. When the paper has been peer reviewed do NOT take offence with the peer reviewers' comments. Answer their comments fully and politely in a covering letter to the editor. You don't have to agree with all their points but you do have to explain why you disagree with them.

9. If the paper is rejected then don't despair, if you have followed the simple rules laid out in this book and are persistent you WILL find somewhere to publish your paper. This should be rule number one – don't give up.

10. Always use as many people to comment on and criticize your paper as possible. Most authors, after the tortured process of conducting their study and writing their paper get very defensive about their 'baby'. Don't! At this stage you have already become the person with the least insight into the paper. Listen to others – they are the voice of truth – unlike that little paranoid voice inside your head.

The remainder of this book expands on these points and describes other ways of increasing your chances of getting into print.

Section 2.　Do you really need to get a paper published?

This really has to be the first question you should ask yourself. Why do you want to get a paper published? There can be a myriad of reasons:

- Career progression
- Personal satisfaction
- To look good in front of your peers/partner/mother
- To begin an academic career
- Because you are interested in a question and want to find out the answer
- Because everyone else is doing it
- Because you have nothing else to do in the evenings.
- Because you have a deep desire to push forward the frontiers of knowledge and to help your fellow man in the process.

Some of these reasons are good and some are bad (I will leave you to figure out which) but none actually matter as long as you really want to do it.

Life is short and summer is shorter. Would you really rather slump over a computer screen than visit your friends, ask your partner about their day, play with your children, go for a walk, visit the cinema or read that piece of great literature you never had the time to?

If you really do want to do the paper after considering more enjoyable options then you have definitely made the first step.

So let's assume from now on that what you start you finish – the worst thing you can do is to do half the job and stop. If you are going to start then make sure you finish.

2.1 Do the journals really need your paper?

Of course the other question you might ask is "Do the journals/science/research/patients need my paper?"

Well the answer is "Yes they do" – for good reasons and bad. Journals obviously need to have papers submitted to them, the more papers they receive the choosier they can be and the choosier they are the better the journals impact factor is (see Section 4.2). This is a little different for open access journals (see Section 4.8) but without doubt journals need papers.

Does science and the research community need your paper? Well again the answer is yes. It is difficult to know in the long term what is going to be important and what isn't. It is easy to look back and recognize important work and it is equally obvious that large multicentre controlled trials are going to be important (whatever they show). What is impossible to be sure about is apparently minor changes in a technique, or an interesting case or hypothesis that turns out to be a crucial turning point. Who would have thought a contaminated agar plate in a London laboratory would be the beginning of antibiotics?

Another argument for publishing is to avoid publication bias. There is a tendency amongst editors (and journalists and administrators, in fact humans in general) to take more notice of 'positive' results. So the study that shows treatment A is much better than treatment B is likely to get noticed and therefore is more likely to end up in a good journal. A different study which shows A and B are no different (or no better than placebo) is much less sexy and will struggle to get into a high profile journal. If the authors become despondent and decide not to submit to another journal then this finding doesn't end up in the literature and this may ultimately mean that the effect of treatment A seems better than it might be simply because of publication bias rather than a real effect.

This has an obvious potential implication for patients. We constantly try to use evidence to inform our practice but if the evidence is biased then what good is it? Over or under estimation of treatment effects can be the result of this publication bias.

So yes, your research, paper or case could be important. If your paper is not important then no-one will look at it, but who knows when it could provide the spark for something more?

Of course a number of papers are not worth cutting down trees to make paper, but nowadays this is less of a worry. Electronic journals both save paper and allow a permanent, easily searchable record of your work. It is a matter of only a few moments for others to find your paper – no longer would they have to search large publications by hand or find references amongst other papers. So there is no excuse, get your work out there! No-one can promise it will be cited more than once but then again no one can guarantee you haven't made history!

Section 3.   Choosing the subject of your publication.

The first thing is to be realistic. If you are new to research and publication then start small with perhaps a case report or a small review. If you are reading this book you are probably not about to embark on a major multicentre randomized trial so a modest beginning is the right step for you.

The best way to find a subject for a paper is to think of a question you are interested in knowing the answer to. If your next patient has condition X and you have never really understood the condition or treatment it is possible others feel the same and an up to date review would be welcome (I will explain what I mean by the word "review" later).

If the patient has condition Z, which is a rarity – or had an unusual presentation or response to treatment, it is worth thinking about putting a Case Report together. We will discuss Case Reports later.

A common way of getting started on the research trail is by doing an audit. You are now thinking, no, I want to do research not an audit. But do you know the difference? Is there a difference? Does it matter? We will discuss audit in a later section and how to differentiate from research, but a well planned and written audit can be an extremely informative piece of work and can definitely change practice. It is often a very good basis for a paper and a good way to get started learning the rules of scientific publication.

If you really don't have any burning questions you want answering and never see unusual patients then ask your colleagues if they have anything they feel is worth looking at. Are there any audits that they are planning to do? Any interesting patients they feel are unique enough to be written up? Often seniors have been asked to write review articles for journals and would appreciate your help with getting references and putting the initial draft together.

This brings us to the subject of Collaborators.

3.1   Choosing your collaborators

You can do the whole thing yourself if you wish but generally speaking collaborators are very useful. Some journal editors are suspicious of papers that come from a single author – unless they contain a review from a person well known in the field.

As well as this there are a number of advantages in collaborating with others to design and implement a study and writing the paper:

- Senior collaborators might have experience of the process and can guide you away from potential pitfalls. They may also be known by the journal you are aiming for – which allows you some inside knowledge of what the publication is looking for.

- Someone to help share the workload.

- Someone who can help to constructively criticize the work.

- Someone to keep you motivated when your interest is flagging.

- Someone to commiserate with when rejection occurs.

- Collaborators give credibility to the work – if you are writing up a series of 100 uses of drug A in condition B and you are the only author, the editor will be somewhat incredulous that you didn't need anyone else's help and that you saw all the patients yourself.

So generally it is good to have collaborators. But be careful, it looks faintly ridiculous to have 23 authors on a paper that discusses a single case of a not very rare disease. The editor will be suspicious that you are either helping out your friends by putting their names on the paper, or that more senior members are exerting influence to 'coat-tail' your work.

The answer? There are specific guidelines that define authorship – we will discuss these in detail in Section 5.2. If you follow these guidelines you won't go far wrong.

For those who haven't had enough involvement to be defined as an Author you can add an acknowledgement section to the paper where they can be named. This is discussed in detail in Section 5.32.

3.2   What type of study do you want to do?

There are a number of study methods that are used to try to gain an insight into a disease or a treatment. There are an even greater number of ways of communicating to the outside world the findings of whichever study you use.

In this section we will describe the various methods of getting into print. It is worth having an idea which one is most appropriate before embarking on your study. It is unlikely you will be reading this book if you are coming towards the end of a Randomized Controlled Trial (RCT) but you will find some pointers as to where and how to get these published. It is more likely you are looking for ANY way to get published and if so you might want to think beyond the normal routes and consider non-peer reviewed publications. They may not be in *PubMed* or look impressive to your academic colleagues but they are a start, and they do show the most important thing for your career – that you are not seen to be standing still.

3.3   Randomized Controlled Trials (RCTs)

Many articles and books have been written about RCTs – if you want to understand their importance have a look at this link:

http://www.bmj.com/cgi/content/full/316/7126/201

For all the things that have been written about RCTs they, more than any study type, exemplify the importance of good study design. If you don't design your RCT properly it WILL go wrong and as well as upsetting a large number of people important to your career, you might never be awarded a grant again.

All the study types mentioned below need good planning and design – if you don't organize the patient's consent for use of an image perhaps it will be too late? If you send your letter to the editor a year after the paper it is commenting on was published it doesn't stand much chance of being accepted.

But this book is not about study design (expect for the fact good studies make good papers and good papers get accepted more than bad ones), it is about getting your study published.

RCTs are collaborative affairs (a single author RCT is fraud – how can you be masked if you are the only person doing the trial?) and therefore it is highly unlikely you won't be supported by a team of people who are well used to publishing trials. Make sure you learn from them – writing up a trial, getting it through peer review, having it published and answering post-publication comments are skills as important to learn as the original study design.

If you are having to write the paper yourself then here are a few tips:

1. Read the general rules about writing a paper described in Section 5

2. Carefully check the rules for submitting an RCT to the journal you have chosen.

3. Unless your particular journal asks you not to use the CONSORT statement then you should. What is the CONSORT statement? It stands for Consolidated Standards of Reporting Trials and was designed to allow a uniformity in the reporting of trials. This is to ensure that important trial information isn't omitted from the paper, making it is easier to assess the quality of the trial. All good journals should ask for RCTs to be published using the CONSORT framework. This can be found, with greater detail here:

http://www.consort-statement.org/

4. Some journals will ask you to submit your CONSORT checklist with your paper. They will also ask for a flow diagram of patients' progress/removal during the trial (this is extremely useful and important). An example of this, from the Archives of Internal Medicine can be seen here:

http://archinte.ama-assn.org/misc/ifora.dtl#References

5. Make sure that the Ethics committee details are in the paper - i.e. the name of the committee and the reference number. Human experimentation must be conducted within the standards set out in the 1975 Declaration of Helsinki. The standards expected in animal experiments differ nationally and it is expected you will give the details of the licenses/

permissions you have for these experiments. For more information look here:

http://www.icmje.org/recommendations/browse/roles-and-responsibilities/protection-of-research-participants.html

6. Put the trial number in the text (this is discussed in more detail later).

Generally speaking, well-conducted and adequately powered (i.e. enough participants to potentially show a real difference between treatments), RCTs are going to be published. They are the most powerful way of discerning efficacy of treatment and can change entire practices. Thus journals are usually very keen to publish them.

If you have ever been involved in an RCT you will understand that the pain and distress of completing the trial is hardly made up by this relatively high level of interest from the journals!

3.4 Laboratory studies

Laboratory research is often thought of as the 'real' science. Test tubes and freezers and white coats are the stereotypes of research. On the other hand there is no reason why other research types, as long as they are properly conducted, should be less valid than laboratory science.

I am not going to discuss much about this type of research, it isn't the sort of thing you are going to do by yourself – as you might a case report or case series. If you are embarking on lab work you will already have made contacts with people who know what they are doing and will (hopefully) be guiding you. You are also likely to be funded – it's hard to set foot in a lab without the guarantee that all your costs are covered. You may think that offering to work for free will be enough, but the person whose budget pays for your reagents, consumables and bench space, probably won't agree.

Similarly it would be hard to imagine that you will be left to write your results and paper by yourself. Labs are full of people who have written many papers and are probably on the editorial boards of journals. They will guide you to the correct journal for your work.

Despite this support and experience, don't assume because they have written a lot of papers they are good at writing them. An awful lot of papers are very poorly written – even those that get published. Stick to the guide in this book – write for your audience, keep it clear and precise and don't try to show how clever you are. Scientific papers can easily get lost in the details of a technique or finding and often this is as it should be, but always try to think of your audience and how you are going to convey the information in your head to theirs.

3.5   Population studies

Like RCTs these are, by definition, well-funded, well-designed (hopefully), multi-author studies. Generally they randomly sample a particular population look at the prevalence of the disease and potential risk factors for the disease.

Again they are likely to be written up by experienced researchers and writers and generally are accepted by the major journals. This is not because they are any 'better' than other types of study but because if the sample is large enough and representative enough the findings could have a major impact on the understanding of a disease.

3.6   Case control (cohort) studies

This type of study compares two populations (cohorts), one with a disease and one without. By looking at various exposures and seeing how they are distributed between cases and controls it might be possible to discern risk factors for the disease. A well known example is the Doll and Peto study that looked at individuals with lung cancer and those without, and ascertained their various exposures – it was this method that uncovered smoking as a cause of lung cancer.

In situations where RCTs can't be conducted (you can't randomly expose one group of people to asbestos and avoid in another group), properly conducted case-control studies can be a very powerful way to investigate causes of disease.

Good, well-designed case control studies are usually well received by journal editors. Poorly designed case-control studies (this usually means poor definition of cases and controls) are not uncommon and are difficult to get published - as one might imagine.

3.7   'Positive' study results

This seems a good time to mention again the permissive influence of positive results. As discussed in Section 2.1, the problems of publication bias and the attraction of positive outcomes to journals are a major cause of this.

We will discuss the distortions caused by Impact Factors later but essentially the Impact Factor is calculated from the number of times a particular article is cited. Thus an article that will change practice is likely to be read by more people than one which doesn't, and therefore will contribute to increasing a journal's Impact Factor.

Editors are therefore – consciously or subconsciously – biased towards studies that produce a positive result (i.e. Drug C was better than Drug D at treating condition X) rather than a negative result (the new treatment Drug F was no better than the old treatment Drug E). There isn't much you can do about this – in fact you shouldn't let it affect your choice of journal. If you do then you are helping to create the publication bias we discussed in Section 2.1. What you should do when writing the paper is to emphasize the important of your results – especially when other papers might have shown a positive effect of the drug. If you are explicit about this in the paper and your covering letter to the Editor you will increase your chances of acceptance.

3.8   Case reports

Traditionally these are the source of the first forays into publication. The reason is that they are simple to write, don't take up too much space, and are popular with readers. They also conveniently 'present' themselves in that they tend to turn up in the ward or clinic one day. It is worth remembering that it is not just the case that might be interesting but the method of presentation or an idiosyncratic response to treatment.

A number of journals have all but discarded case reports on the basis that they can influence practice disproportionately. One case/treatment described going wrong can seem to be more influential than large RCTs! However, whether related to this or not, a number of journals in the last few years have emerged which publish case reports only. Some of these are shown below with their URL.

International Medical Case Reports journal:

http://www.dovepress.com/international-medical-case-reports-journal-journal

The Journal of Medical Case Reports:

http://jmedicalcasereports.com/

BMJ Case Reports:

http://casereports.bmj.com/

So there are quite a number of case report journals to choose from, as well as many established journals that remain happy to accept this sort of paper. Generally the more specialist journals carry more case reports, but as you can see from the list above, the more general journals are attempting to create their own case reports' specialisations. Again check with the "instructions for authors" section of the journal you intend to submit to. If they mention that they don't like single case reports then don't waste your time submitting to them – there are plenty of other choices.

Once you have found a journal that does accept case reports check carefully the format and style the journal wants them presented in. There are some general rules to adhere to that will increase your chance of having the paper accepted:

1. To repeat – check the "instructions for authors" before submitting the paper.

2. Remember this is a patient you are describing not a case. Many journals ask for the patient's consent before publishing a case, especially if it contains images. But it is good practice,

no matter what the policy of the journal, to tell the patient what you intend to do and make sure they have no objections.

3. If you are submitting images remember there may be a charge for these – it can be quite substantial if there are a lot of colored photographs.

4. Try to describe the case concisely but with necessary detail. Conclude by saying what the reader can learn from the case – this is what the reader really wants.

3.9   Case series

Of course if you can find a series of cases – again either an unusual condition or presentation or response to treatment – even better. Editors are more interested in the illustrative power of more than one case.

Having said that, most journals treat case reports and case series the same way so stick to the same rules described above. If you have a large number of cases then individual patient consent is not practical, although if a patient is potentially identifiable from either a description or an illustration, do get their consent to publish.

3.10   Reviews, perspectives

If the thought of original research seems too daunting, a review of a subject or area or treatment can be popular with journals. Different journals give these pieces different names but essentially they provide a comprehensive, up to date review of a topic of interest for readers.

Some journals commission these pieces and it is worth asking your seniors or colleagues if they have been asked to do a review.

Volunteering to get hold of the references and to make a start with the writing tends to go down well.

Journals may be amenable to being approached with suggestions for reviews. Again it depends upon the journal but to increase your chances of acceptance, the following points might help:

- Check if the journal you have chosen does take this type of article.

- Make sure the area you want to write about has not recently been reviewed in the journal (check back a few years).

- Be specific, don't say you want to write a review on 'Heart disease'.

- Write to the editor with a brief outline of the review you want to write, why it might be interesting to the readers, how long it will be, and why now is the time to write it.

- Explain why you (and your collaborators) are the right people to do this review.

- Give an indication of how long it will take you to finish the review and make sure it is possible. It looks very bad to be chased for a paper that you yourself had initially suggested writing.

3.11   Editorials

Editorials are almost always written by experts in the field. They are usually related to a particular article in a journal or to a particular topical issue that might be pertinent to the journal's specialty.

Generally the editor will identify someone who is qualified to write an editorial and will contact them. For obvious reasons this is likely to be a more senior member of your department, but as with reviews they are often grateful for help with references and initial drafts. Ask around your department, has anyone been asked to do an editorial? If so, approach them with an offer of help.

It is also possible to contact an editor and suggest an idea for an editorial. This needs to be 'sold' well to the editor – you will need to convince them that an editorial would be worthwhile. The way to convince them is similar to that for reviews:

- The editor wants an editorial that will be read and provoke debate amongst the readers. So make it a relevant subject – one you know that your peers are already taking about. Carefully explain to the editor the relevance and pertinence of the subject you are proposing.

- Explain to the editor why you and your colleague(s) are the people who should be writing the Editorial

- Promise a time when it will be ready – editorials are by nature usually timely.

3.12   Cochrane (and other systematic) Reviews

In the hierarchy of evidence that effects practice, Cochrane reviews sit on top of the pile. The reason for this is that they summarize the available evidence for an intervention in a highly systematic and rigorous fashion.

You have probably heard of the term systematic review and it simply means using explicit criteria to judge the quality of studies and to decide if the study (usually an RCT) is of an acceptable methodological quality. All studies that fulfill these criteria can then be 'lumped together' and analyzed (called a meta-analysis) to produce an overall recommendation. A treatment or intervention might be shown to be valuable or harmful, or there may not be evidence one way or another.

There are other systematic reviews that are not Cochrane – which can cause confusion - but the methodology of the Cochrane reviews is so explicit and detailed that they really are the 'best' evidence for a treatment's effect.

This quality means that to do a Cochrane review is a rigorous undertaking. Quite naturally if you have a clinical question (which is what drives the Cochrane reviews) you will want to put together the highest quality evidence to answer the question. Depending upon your specialty or area of interest, you can approach your appropriate Cochrane review group. They are listed here on the Cochrane website:

http://www.cochrane.org/contact/review-groups

When you find the group most appropriate for your question you can then register a title by writing a short proposal, and if this title is agreed then you proceed to put together a Protocol. This is a detailed description of your question(s), essential background detail, how you will search for appropriate papers and how you will deal with the results. This is peer reviewed and then you proceed to do the full review.

Sounds easy? Well it isn't. Cochrane reviews are extremely valuable and important – they can change an entire practice overnight. So they have to be highly rigorous – all relevant papers need to be found and read to see if there are any flaws (e.g. poor randomization technique, lack of explicit detail of how trials patients were selected) that might cast doubt on the validity of the results. Meta-analysis doesn't just involve adding all the patients from the different studies together – studies are heterogeneous and you need to allow for this. Assessing whether primary and secondary questions have been answered is again complex. I could go on. Completing a Cochrane review is good for your career, kudos and self esteem but, like all things of quality, it comes at a price.

If you have read my warnings above and STILL think you want to do a Cochrane review then make sure you can put a tick beside all the points below. If you can then go ahead and find a Review Group and see if they are interested:

1. Make sure you have a clinical question that you REALLY want to know the answer to – this will keep you going on the dark days.

2. Plan to stay in the specialty – Cochrane reviews are not one-off pieces of work. Evidence is constantly accumulating and needs to be searched and added regularly. New trials could change the review's conclusions and indeed change clinical practice forever. So think carefully. Can you commit to regular updates of your review? If you are not planning to stay in a specialty then it may be best not to embark on a review. If you do, make sure your co-reviewers will be able to continue.

3. Collaborators – you can't actually do a Cochrane review yourself, its structure requires at least one collaborator. If you can have more than one collaborator, do so. The work can be divided up. If your collaborator has experience of reviews or of evidence based medicine then so much the better. Remember though that reviews are not one-offs and you need to ensure that your collaborators are people you can work with in the long term.

4. Time – reviews are high(est) quality information and analysis and it takes time to plan, search for papers, read the papers and put the papers together. If you don't feel you have this time (it is a full time job for some people) then don't start.

As a general rule, don't start things you can't finish (except CPR), it irritates the hell out of people.

5. Facilities – you will need access to computers with broadband Internet facility and a library. Increasingly your library can be online but this can make it expensive to purchase papers, and you may not know how relevant they are until you have paid for them. Ideally you should have a medical library nearby and have practiced being very nice to the librarian.

6. Dogged determination – this is an absolutely crucial quality needed to complete a review. If you haven't got this then go swimming instead – though I suggest you avoid the deep end.

3.13 Audits

If you have never heard anyone say 'it's not research, its only audit' then you soon will. There seems to be a desperate attempt to separate them with the implication that audit is a poor second. This seems a shame as good audits can be very powerful tools for changing practice.

There is some confusion as to the difference between audit and research and most people you ask will have their own definitions (and disagree with everyone else's). For me the difference is simply that research is new and audit is review.

Research is looking into areas or having ideas that are novel – it may be treatments, causality, risk factors – it doesn't really matter. It can also involve trying to replicate others work to confirm or refute it so there is some looseness about the word 'new'. Audit on the other hand is devising a way of measuring adherence to already established treatments, mechanisms, processes and seeing if they are working correctly and efficiently. If an audit shows a system is not working then changes can be made and re-audited – with ideally an improved outcome.

Audits can be used at an individual level (e.g. comparison of an individual's surgical results with the 'Gold Standard') or unit level (e.g. overall mortality rate for a unit compared to average national rates) or national level (e.g. patients with CJD compared to international averages). They can be used to assess and monitor almost any aspect of practice from hand hygiene policy adherence to neonatal deaths. So really the phrase 'just an audit' is only true if the subject for the audit is chosen poorly or the audit is badly designed or is not acted upon if adverse results are shown.

There are more practical differences between audit and research and these differences can be useful to the fledgling practitioner. These will vary from country to country and even from institution to institution, so do check with your local Research Board or Committee first. As mentioned, if the definition of research is 'new', then generally speaking a research protocol has to be reviewed and accepted by an Ethical Committee and in many places a Research Board. As research is essentially experimentation the Ethics Committee need to be sure that participants are not exposed to unjustifiable risks (even if it is other members of staff who are the subjects, the Ethics committee will want to evaluate any risks or coercion) and that the researchers are capable of running an ethical study. The Research Board wants to make sure that the study is appropriate for the institution and the individuals who are conducting the study, and that the finances are in place.

If you have had to go through this process you will have found it time-consuming and frustrating. If the Ethical Committee question you about the study this seems like an unnecessary delay as does the institution's Research Board's query about who will pay for the blood tests etc. These are not superfluous questions and they are not out to get you (all researchers become paranoid – for lots of reasons, just get used to it and don't let it affect your judgment) but it can seem to take a long time even to get permission to begin your study. If you are only in a department or region for a short time it is almost impossible to initiate and conduct a research study.

Audit on the other hand, being simply a review of current practice as compared to a Gold Standard (which of course could itself have been created using research) does not need Ethical or Research Board approval. I have to repeat again, that this is not always true and I do know of some institutions that require formal submissions before an audit can begin. Many institutions have formal audit systems where ideas for audits are sent and checked for relevance and any financial issues (e.g. getting patients' records). You should check this before you start your audit, but it is usually a much simpler process than ethical approval.

You can see that audits are much easier to fit into a limited timescale. As pretty much anything can be audited there are lots of processes to choose from. Audit should be part of our routine practice now and departments should be showing that they are auditing their work. If the subject of an audit is not obvious to you (e.g. an area of interest or a recent national gold standard that was published) speak to your colleague or seniors – they are likely to have some suggestions. It is essential to have backing of your seniors for the audit – not only do they know the areas that need auditing but their influence will be helpful when trying to get patients' notes. If you have to present findings that show underperformance in an area you will also need all the friends you can get!

To some extent the distinction between research and audit is artificial (hence the difficulty in separating the definitions). Audit can be novel and have findings that have never been published before whilst some research is simply the publication of the results of an individual's daily practice. So don't worry too much if you can't decide what you are planning to do is research or audit. If you are planning something that no-one else has done before then accept you will have to go through an Ethics Committee etc. If you are simply re-looking at an audit from a few years before then there is no need to do anything more than let the audit committee know your plans and method. If you are not sure which category your work will fit into then just ask – your colleagues might know, especially senior ones who are experienced. An email to the head of the Ethics Committee and/or Research Board asking their advice can be the simplest and most effective way.

Remember that, like research, audits need to be planned, conducted, analyzed and reported rigorously. If you simply think it's 'only' an audit you could well end up in a mess. Audits can be very powerful tools:

http://www.ncbi.nlm.nih.gov/pmc/articles/PMC1114391/

Like any powerful tool treat it with respect. The details of how to properly conduct audits are beyond the scope of this book but for further information have a look at these sites:

http://www.rcpsych.ac.uk/pdf/clinauditChap1.pdf

http://www.uhbristol.nhs.uk/files/nhs-ubht/1%20What%20 is%20Clinical%20Audit%20v3.pdf

Although doing an audit is less complex than research, getting your audit published tends to be more difficult. It is not hard to see why – journals want papers that describe new work, not how you or your departments compare to your colleagues. But if you have conducted a high-quality audit and the results are relevant

– especially if they show that a change of practice produced an improved outcome - then there is a good chance of publication.

To improve your chance of publication, here are a few hints:

- Choose your journal carefully -make sure they publish audits.

- As with research write the paper coherently and accurately. Explain the relevance of your audit and its findings and how they will change practice.

- Don't try to hide the fact that you are reporting an audit by using overly scientific language, inappropriately complex statistics etc.

- Similarly, don't overstate your findings.

- In your covering letter to the Editor explain why you are submitting an audit for publication and why the readers will be interested in it.

3.14 Letters to the Editor

A relatively rapid way of gaining a publication is a 'Letter to the Editor'. There are two types of these, depending on the journal's policy.

1. Some journals will publish short communications (case reports, case series, equipment or surgical techniques, patient safety reports etc.). These tend to be in the larger journals and have a strict word limit. They are usually pieces that the editor thinks would be of some interest to the reader but doesn't feel warrants the space of a whole paper.

   Sometimes you will submit your paper and after peer review the editor will offer publication but only if you trim it down to a short communication/letter to the editor. You must decide if you and your co-authors want to accept this or resubmit somewhere else. I must admit that I generally accept the offer - the paper will usually be indexed in the same way as a full paper, and whilst it may not be so widely noticed you will at leas have a publication in that journal. Possibly the commonest reason for agreeing to this is fatigue and simply not wanting to go through the whole peer review process again with another journal!

2. The other type of letter to the editor is in response to a paper published in the journal. The advantages of this are (i) that you don't have to think up a topic for your publication yourself and (ii) that editors are generally keen on such submissions because they stir up debate in their journal. They are expected to be short pieces and to the point.

    The disadvantages are that editors know that some letters are written simply to get into a publication rather than make a point, or to insert one's own results in under the disguise of discussing someone else's.

3. The letter needs to be well written (i.e. no wasted words) and to be relevant to the paper it is commenting upon. For example you might suggest that there is a flaw in the study design or analysis or that the conclusions are not appropriate for the results. These points are important as they may alter how the paper is perceived by readers. Treat a letter to the editor with as much care as any other publication, write scientifically but clearly and make your points logically. Get it checked by colleagues before you submit and make sure they agree that your comments are measured and reasonable. The journal will not publish a rant or anything personal or anything libellous.

    Most journals now have electronic submissions of these letters and some display them on their website. It is a confusing grey area if these 'eletters' are actual publications or not. The *British Medical Journal* for example only considers the rapid responses that are selected for print publication as official publications. Purely electronic journals would of course count eletters as official publications as this is the only format used. You could check on *PubMed* to see if the eletters from a journal are listed. Even if they are not, there is nothing wrong with putting them on your CV/Resumé as long as you indicate they are eletters.

3.15   Non-peer reviewed articles

There are a number of outlets for articles that are not peer reviewed prior to publication (though they may be edited). There are many controversies about peer review and arguments for and against. However, like democracy, it is probably the least worst system we have – and it is, whether we like it or not, the system we are stuck with.

The words 'peer review' have now transcended their original meaning and have attained one of their own – that a paper is a good/important one. The converse of this being that a paper that is not peer-reviewed is of poor quality or not so important.

Those who have experience of the peer review system know neither of these to be necessarily true – some very dodgy papers can get through peer review whilst high quality work is rejected. The reasons for this are legion and we won't go into them here, but peer review does not guarantee quality and just because a paper or article isn't peer reviewed doesn't mean it doesn't have an important message.

If you don't want to go through the rigors of peer review then there are a number of options you can choose from including:

- Advertising-funded journals – there are a number of these journals, mainly medical, as this is where the advertising money is. They generally are looking for articles and case reports so there is a good chance of acceptance for a well written, relevant article. Contact the editor and send an outline of the article you wish to submit. Although it will not be peer reviewed it will be edited. Not only can these articles be very useful to the readers, the wide circulation (they are generally free as the advertising pays) can mean that the article has more of an 'impact' than other formats.

- Institutional journals - some institutions produce their own publications, with a limited circulation. Again although lower down the pecking order of publication it may get you noticed by the people who matter to you.

- Online journals – by this I don't mean peer reviewed, electronic-only journals, which are exactly the same as print journals in everything except their physical format. There are some journals which exist online and are not peer reviewed – they are the equivalent of the advertising-paid journals discussed in the previous section. Again they are keen for articles so you have a good chance of acceptance. It is much harder to be sure that the people you want to be reading your work are actually reading it, though in compensation you will have a potentially worldwide audience. A quick online search should reveal some of these online journals in your own specialty.

- Blogs and forums – these are discussed below.

Which of the above you decide to opt for depends on yourself, your situation, the media in which you are most comfortable and the experience of your colleagues and seniors.

There is no reason why these articles shouldn't go into your CV/Resumé as a 'publication'. If the definition of a publication is that it is listed in the major databases (such as *PubMed*, *Web of Science, Scopus, Psycinfo, OAIster*) then you wouldn't be able to call it a publication. But there are actually no 'rules' as such and having something published is better than an empty box on your CV.

Researching the article itself is as much a skill as is learning to write in a coherent scientific fashion. You will learn more about the subject you are writing about as you turn yourself into a temporary expert. Who knows, someone may see your article and ask you to expand and enhance it for a peer reviewed journal. They certainly won't do that if the paper is sitting in a drawer in your office.

If it is only your CV you are concerned about then it really is better to have shown you have been active. Interviewers like to see that you have at least tried and know from their own experience that having a publication isn't really that hard if you try!

3.16   Other routes to getting 'published'

There are of course other methods of getting your message out there and if you are looking for less formal methods you can consider them. They are certainly valid and popular methods of communication but in the relatively conservative world of science and medicine you will have to decide how others perceive their importance.

Some examples include:

Blogs – these are of course increasingly popular ways of getting your thoughts into the public domain. Whether anyone is listening or not is another thing.

If you are a well known name it is obviously more likely you will be followed. If you know virtually nothing about a subject as you are relatively new to it then it will be harder for others to see value in your thoughts.

Starting from scratch will be a slow process, but if you can provide useful content, enjoyable reading and you persist then you will slowly pick up followers. Self-publicity helps and how brassnecked you want to be is entirely your decision.

If simply getting something onto your CV for the next job is your aim then a blog is a simple way to get started. At the very least it shows you are trying to do something. That's better than nothing – but only just.

Videos – with the increase in memory capacity and bandwidth there are an increasing number of sites where you can upload videos of practice. These, by their nature, are biased toward procedures, but there is no reason that you can't upload single interesting pictures.

Again these are generally thought of as fairly low in the hierarchy of research activity (they are not really research) but they are still activity. Done properly and with a little bit of subtly viral 'marketing' they can be useful and popular.

Forums – there are also an increasing number of sites that promote discussion between practitioners and these can be very instructive. Regular postings can get you noticed. It might be worth becoming a moderator of a forum – which can look good.

If you litter your CV with words like *Twitter*, *Facebook* etc. you might be lucky in your interview and get some old fuddy-duddy (like me) who is vaguely fearful of these sites and is impressed by your apparent mastery of them.

That's a long shot though, but running a forum is so much easier than writing a paper.

However on the assumption that you are going to aim for a 'proper' paper in a journal read on......

Section 4.   Choosing your journal

It is likely that you have a vague idea already of the journal that you might submit your paper to. You will be aware of the journals in your field and perhaps have some idea of the types of paper they accept.

You will also most likely have a greater opinion of the importance of your own work than the editor of the journal will. Look at the paper you want to write and be realistic. You can submit it to whichever journal you wish but have you really got the time or the heart to keep on submitting and getting rejected? I suspect not. So think carefully about your journal and how your article might fit into it so you can reduce the chances of rejection. These points will help in this choice:

4.1   Your audience

Again, you will probably have some idea of who you are writing for. If you don't then possibly you shouldn't be writing.

Spend some time in the library or online looking at the journals in your area. There are some websites which list the journals of each specialty:

http://www.medbioworld.com/

http://www.sciencedirect.com/

You can get some idea of the aims and scope from the journals. It is likely to be described on their webpage or within the print journal. Avoid the more obvious errors such as submitting to a journal outside your own specialty but there are often other clues such as not accepting case reports or a journal full of basic science that should indicate the suitability or not of your paper.

4.2   What you need this paper FOR?

Do you want an academic career where you are judged on your ability to get research into the 'best' journals, or do you simply want to get at least one entry under the heading 'Publications' on your CV?

Well if you want the former you are looking for a journal with a high Impact Factor. What is an impact factor and why does everyone keep mentioning it? Impact factor was designed to give a numerical value to the 'worth' of a journal. How is a journal's worth measured? It is assumed that the more important a paper is the more often it is cited by other papers. Similarly the more papers that a journal has that are heavily cited the more influential the journal is i.e. the more *impact* the journal has.

This Impact Factor is calculated using the number of citations to articles divided by the total number of articles in a particular journal over a set time. *Thomson Reuters* publish the 'official' impact factor but only certain journals are tracked and new journals are not usually included until five years after initial publication.

There are many criticisms of Impact Factor – is it really measuring the true importance of a journal? If a bad paper gets into a high impact journal it is perceived as better than it actually is and the impact factor can be manipulated. Whatever its drawbacks, there is no doubt that Impact Factor is seen as a marker of worth for a journal and for researchers. Like peer review it has become almost mythical in its importance to institutions and funders. This becomes self-perpetuating as the journals want the best (i.e the most likely to be cited) papers which then improve their impact factor, which attracts the best papers etc.

Unsurprisingly it is difficult to be published in a high impact factor journal unless your study really is important. You can find the impact factor of a journal from its webpage – if it doesn't have one then it is either too new or is not deemed worthy of being tracked by *Thomson*. If you do need to publish in a high impact journal then you will need plenty of advice and support from those more used to the process.

Journal 'prestige' is another factor that may have a bearing upon your decisions - although an intangible one. Impact factor undoubtedly has a bearing on this but some journals have a prestige within a research or practice area that is not reflected in their impact factor.

Similarly, some journals have a very low impact factor because they represent a small area of practice. But they are read by most members of that small area so in reality they do have a much bigger (real) impact. These are often the best sort of journals to publish in when you are getting started. They will get you noticed amongst the people you want to be noticed by.

Try to put impact factor and prestige out of your mind and try to get your paper into the journal where it fits best and which is appropriate for the content. This might mean a prestigious journal, but be led by how good the paper is not by how good the journal is. Also, remember you will overestimate the importance and interest of your paper, so get someone experienced to look at it and guide you on its true relevance and the journal to which it would most likely be suited.

4.3   Type of article

To some extent, the type of paper you are writing will suggest a journal. If you have decided to go down the non-peer reviewed route (see below) this obviously discounts a large number of journals. Conversely if you have discovered a gene for a disease then you are entitled to aim for a high impact journal.

Some types of journal actually tell you what papers they want (case report journals tend to be called just that), some journals just publish review articles.

4.4   Peer reviewed or not?

I won't go into the rights or wrongs of peer review here – as I mentioned before, my personal feeling is that peer review is similar to Winston Churchill's views of democracy. There is no getting away from the fact though that peer review does add a certain kudos to your paper. It is like a quality mark stamped on your work.

Whether this is fair or not is a different matter, but peer review is one of those 'sheep and goats' processes where it is easy to separate 'good' from 'bad' by using external criteria (researchers love doing this as it saves having to read the paper). Needless to say there are some great papers that are not peer reviewed and some awful ones that have been peer reviewed (though one wonders by whom!).

There are advantages and disadvantages to submitting to a peer reviewed journal:

Advantages

- The journal (and therefore paper) is deemed to have a mark of quality.

- You will get a high quality review of your paper (accepted or not) for free.

- It is a method of protecting the research world from fraud. Unfortunately not always a successful method.

Disadvantages

- It takes time. It is usually the commonest delay in the whole process of publication.

- Peer reviewers are human and can make mistakes.

- They can also be your competitors and try to block your work for their own ends.

Where the balance of a decision lies to submit to a peer-reviewed journal or not depends on your needs from the paper and your collaborators' views.

4.5   Indexed journals.

Related to the status of a journal is whether it is indexed in the various academic databases. As there are now a huge number of journals covering a wide range of specialties, sub-specialties and niches it is impossible for anyone to be aware of even a fraction of their content. Therefore a number of databases have been developed which index these papers, and there are now a huge number of databases! Some cover many disciplines, some only one, some are free whilst others require subscription.

You may be aware of your own specialist database – the commonest biomedical database is *PubMed*, for psychology it is *PsycINFo*, for economics *Econlit*, for law *Westlaw*. There are many more and the vast majority can easily be searched online or through *Google Scholar* – which itself includes a huge number of citations.

To find out if the journal you intend to submit to has been accepted by an indexer you can either look at the journals website or check on the appropriate database's website. All have somewhere that lists the journals that they contain.

Remember that it takes time for a new journal to be accepted by an indexer and for a paper to be added to the indexer's database. If you are submitting to a relatively new journal it may or may not have been accepted by the database or it might be awaiting upload of its first papers. Check with the journal's website or you can email the editorial staff and ask.

4.6   Electronic versus print journals

This probably won't have a great affect on your decision. Print journals do tend to be the older more established journals but the majority now have an electronic version. I have no doubt that for economic reasons all journals will eventually become electronic – though many people prefer to read from paper rather than from a screen. Most journals now have electronic submission – which we will discuss later.

Whether you think there are ethical issues about chopping down trees to print some information that only a handful of people will read is up to you. What electronic journals do allow is the ability to write a more detailed paper – there are no limits on size that print journals by necessity have. This can also mean that you can add more illustrations or videos or references. The references themselves can be hyperlinked to the articles – very useful for your readers.

Your librarian will be pleased if you choose an electronic journal – it means more shelf-space!

One concern that people have is the permanence of journals – like any business they can go bust and it is possible (especially if the journal does not deposit copies with the indexer) that your paper could disappear. At least if it was in a hard copy it could be archived somewhere. Having said that I have never been aware of a case of this yet happening.

4.7   Unknown factors

Finally there are certain intangibles over which you have no control, and even worse it's likely you will know nothing about. These are the reasons that perfectly good papers that have good peer reviews are rejected by journals. They are also the reasons why, to contradict the title of this book, it is impossible to guarantee publication for all papers.

Some reasons for this apparent arbitrariness are (i) a backlog of papers awaiting publication (there is no point publishing a trial 2 years late), (ii) there may be a new ambitious editor who wants to increase the journal's impact factor and is discarding all but the very 'best' papers, (iii) some print journals have a limit on the size of the journal they can produce because of cost, (iv) decisions are made by humans and not machines, the editor might hate your co-author so much that their one aim in life is to prevent any of their papers being published.

You can see that the process of having a paper accepted for publication is not as rigorous and logical as you thought – so if you do get rejected don't take it personally (though maybe you should?!)

4.8   Open Access Journals

A word about open access (OA) journals. It has long been thought by those who are outside the major publishing companies that there is an issue about access to scientific papers. A study that has been publicly funded is then published in a journal which requires either a subscription to that journal or a large amount of dollars to download the paper. Of course this is how the publishers make their profits but it also means that potentially useful information comes at a cost and may therefore reduce accessibility.

To try to remedy this situation, some journals now have an open access system where papers are free to download in their entirety. Who pays for this? Well the author pays a one-off fee – a publication or administration fee – that allows free access for the paper in perpetuity. The advantages to the reader are obvious, to the patient are positive and to the author are also positive – open access journals have been shown to be cited more than closed access. The reason for this is probably the easier access to the paper.

A number of publishers are now fully open access:

Dove Medical Press - www.dovepress.com

Biomed Central – www.biomedcentral.com

Whilst others have some papers open and some closed:

British Medical Journal:

http://resources.bmj.com/bmj/authors/types-of-article

Others, such as the *Journal of the American Medical Association* (JAMA) have a more complex model with a limited number of open access papers in a time period but complete open access to readers from developing countries. Other journals allow the author to choose to pay for OA publication – if he decides not to then the article is published as subscription-only access.

How much this publication fee is varies widely between journals. If you prefer to publish in an OA journal you can check the fees on the journal's website. Most journals will provide a waiver of the fee if you are from an economically developing country – again check on the journal's website. Contact the editorial office of the journal if you have any queries about this. Whatever you do DON'T submit to an OA journal and then find you can't pay the fee when the time comes – this will be when the paper is ready for publication, so it is not only you who will be frustrated.

A number of sponsors of research will provide funds for their recipients to publish in open access journals – increasingly some funders insist upon this. This is hardly surprising. If public money has funded research then the public and their practitioners should have free access to the results of this research. If you are a funded researcher check if your grant awarding body provides fees for OA publication.

At present, whether a journal is OA probably doesn't have a lot of bearing on someone's decision to submit to that journal. Other factors, discussed previously, such as prestige, impact factor and appropriateness of the journal are much more influential in the decision. However, some authors do want to publish OA as they feel it is the correct route, others are bound to by their funders. OA publishing has its critics and proponents and we will see how it develops in the future.

Your decision about the type of journal you decide to submit to will depend on a combination of the above. If you are in doubt about any aspect of a journal's policy (e.g. peer review) then ask – far better to do this before you submit. Your colleagues will likely have valuable advice – if there is an academic department nearby they are likely to have an idea of the appropriateness of various journals.

You can approach the journals directly – there is nothing wrong with emailing an editor and asking if your work would be suitable for their journal. For some types of papers such as large reviews/ perspectives and uncommissioned editorials this is mandatory. Many editors welcome this approach as it can save them time if your paper is not suitable. Don't email the whole paper, just give an indication or outline of your work.

Section 5.   Writing your paper

Unsurprisingly the quality of writing of your paper is the most important determinant of whether it will be accepted for publication or not. Even the most specialty-changing trial will struggle to be published if it is unreadable. So spend time getting it right and pay attention to detail.

This section will explain how to enhance the writing of your paper and therefore vastly increase its chance of being published. Written communication is just that – *communication*. You need to stick to the conventions of the journal you select and the general conventions of scientific writing, but within those parameters also think of the reader. The more readable a paper is, the more the words flow, the greater the impression it will make on the reader.

We will discuss this in more depth in the forthcoming sections.

5.1   Instructions for authors

I have repeated *ad nauseam* the importance of reading the "Instructions for Authors" before you submit a paper. It is amazing how many authors don't.

Although the standard structure of a paper is the model that most use, almost all journals have their own particular rules. This may vary from their own format, to maximum word limit, to the structure of the abstract to statements of conflict of interest. But none of these are secrets - the word *Instruction* is a clue.

In most journals these rules are located on the submission page for electronic submission, or for purely print journals, are found inside the journal.

If you don't adhere to these instructions it is most likely that the paper will be returned to you immediately. It is very irritating when you finally get your paper sent off and feel you can relax for a while, but instead it comes winging its way straight back for simple corrections.

The huge number of manuscripts received by many good journals means that they look for any reason to reject a paper (though this is not always true – see the section on Print versus Electronic journals). Don't give the editor an easy way of dismissing you by showing that you can't even read simple instructions.

Once again, in case I haven't been clear **READ THE INSTRUCTIONS FOR AUTHORS BEFORE YOU START WRITING THE PAPER.**

5.2   Authors and authorship

This is a surprisingly controversial area. Superficially it would seem self-evident whose names should be on the paper. Unfortunately – and you may find this yourself –it is not quite that simple.

There are numerous reasons why some people are listed as authors without earning this right. Unfortunately one of the crude ways we measure the research pedigree of an individual is by how many papers they have published. Thus departmental heads who have had nothing to do with the paper insist on authorship, co-workers who promise to put your name on their own paper are added, and protégés who need a help getting on the ladder are named.

In response to these abuses the *International Committee of Medical Journal Editors* (ICMJE) has put together guidelines that define authorship. These are extremely useful if you are having trouble establishing this. They can be viewed here:

http://www.icmje.org/recommendations/browse/roles-and-responsibilities/defining-the-role-of-authors-and-contributors.html

Some journals actually ask you to make a statement about authorship during submission – and some publish it with the paper. Even if the journal you are submitting to doesn't ask this, it is good practice to add it yourself. The ICJME link will give you a useful template to copy if you need to construct one of your own.

5.3   Language

Most medical journals are written in English and it has been said that English is the dominant language of science and medicine. Such is the dominance of the USA and UK that the vast majority of the more influential journals are written in English. There is also a huge bias towards citation of English language journals and it has been recognized that many non-English language papers are not widely read or cited. This can lead to publication bias (both by ignoring studies that may affect meta-analyses and not including different ethnic groups in results). The Cochrane Collaboration has long recognized this and has tried hard to include non-English trials in their searches.

If you do want to get your paper into an English language journal but your first language isn't English then you need to think carefully. Editors are always looking for ways to quickly reduce the deluge of papers sent to them and if the English in a paper is poor they will reject it out of hand. There are a number of things to consider:

1. Do you really need to submit to an English language journal? Who is your audience? If it is mainly your colleagues is there an advantage in publishing in an English journal?

2. Is your English good enough to write the paper?

3. If it isn't, you really do need a native English speaker to check the accuracy of the language in the paper.

4. Ideally this will be a co-author but if not they should be acknowledged in the paper.

5. There are professional services that can correct the paper for you although these can be expensive.

6. Some journals provide this service and it is worth asking, before you submit, if they would be able to 'polish' the manuscript. This might also alert them to possible language difficulties in your paper that might help in the peer review process.

5.4   Grammar and spelling

It is not only non-native English speakers who can write unintelligible papers. Plenty of native speakers write with such poor grammar that the paper is difficult to read. It is the quickest way to receive the paper back in your inbox. Even if it does evade the editor's notice and is sent for peer review, the reviewers will get very irate if the grammar or spelling is poor.

The peer reviewers are (voluntarily) assessing whether your paper is worthy of publication and if you want to increase the chances of a favorable opinion make an effort to make your paper easy to read. Even the most groundbreaking piece of research will struggle to get published if the peer reviewers can't wade through it. We will discuss this more in the next section but there is a way of making any written work more readable and this begins by sticking to the conventions of the language structure.

There isn't any excuse for poor grammar or spelling mistakes when you were born and educated in the language. For those who rely on automated means, spell checks on word processing should eradicate these completely. It is also worth using the grammar function. Whilst this is not fail-safe it can be useful in picking up your more glaring errors.

However, don't use these word processing correctors to avoid writing the paper properly in the first place, and don't think that because it is a scientific paper the rules of English do not apply. Arguably they are MORE important as you are trying to put over some complex concepts and you don't want poor grammar to get in the way of this.

As with all writing after one or two rewrites it becomes difficult for your brain to see the errors - it tends to see what it thinks is there rather than what is actually there. Ask someone who has never read the paper before to go over it – you will be surprised by how many howlers they uncover.

For the definitive guide to the rules of writing I suggest you get the *Elements of Style* by William Strunk and E.B. White (see the "Resources for Authors" section for details).

5.5   Narrative

It might seem odd to talk about narrative in a book about scientific papers. What have stories got to do with science?

Well, humans communicate by stories - if a string of information doesn't make sense, if it is in the wrong order, if one step doesn't follow from another, if there is no obvious beginning or context or end then our minds struggle to make sense of the information. So if you want someone to understand your message then you have to write in a narrative form. Why else do you think novels are the most widely read books?

Of course a scientific paper is not Fitzgerald or Dickens (although it probably could be Hemingway) and it needs precision and accuracy. But its essential nature is to communicate a message and it needs to have an internal logic. In fact the standard structure of a scientific paper already contains a logical sequence of steps.

As I will discuss later, the paper is essentially a why, how and what happened – just like a novel. The introduction to the paper sets the scene for the reader – what has gone before and where we are now - and then begins to suggest where we are going. The method section tells us how we are going to get to our destination, the results what we found as we travelled and arrived and the discussion tells us what it all means, how the results fit in with others' findings and what the next steps should be.

When you are writing your paper don't try to show off to the reader how clever you are by using technical language or long sentences. Nor assume their understanding of complex background details. Don't write in a languid style as if you are the Great Man of Science who is spreading pearls of wisdom. How to do this? Stick to these rules:

1. Don't use more words than you need to. This is not easy and requires numerous rewrites. Rewrites should invariably

remove words not add them. The art of writing a paper is to distil the essential information.

2. Write in the active voice not passive (see next section).

3. Don't show off, write as if it really matters to you that the reader understands your message.

4. Make sure you write in a logical fashion i.e. the next sentence, next paragraph and next section follow on from the previous one without the reader having to look back and check.

5. Don't write in a patronizing manner but don't assume the reader understands everything you are writing about. You don't need to explain everything, a reference will suffice so that the reader can check it themselves if they wish.

6. Always get your paper checked by as many people as possible before you submit. If possible get a non-specialist to read it – they will focus more on the readability of the paper rather than the detail, and this will be very helpful.

7. If you do have to put in a lot of technical detail (such as laboratory techniques or patient classification criteria) try to avoid distracting the reader. If the journal has the facility you may be able to put this detail on its webpage and give a link in the paper. If the detail is to be included in the printed journal consider putting it into a separate box – the reader can then choose to refer to this or not.

8. As discussed above, make sure you spend time getting the grammar correct. There is nothing so difficult to read as tortured, non-grammatical sentences.

5.6   Passive and active voice

You may not be aware that amongst the many divisions and clauses of the English grammatical structure are the passive and active voices. These are much more important than you think – and you use them constantly without realizing it. They are of particular importance in writing – especially technical and scientific writing.

Active and passive have nothing to do with tenses but they are a way of ordering words to convey a message. An active sentence is where the doer of the action is the subject of the sentence. For example:

I received your manuscript today.

This is a straightforward punchy sentence that mentions the doer (I) then the action (received) and then the noun (manuscript).

The alternative to this illustrates the passive voice:

Your manuscript was received by me today

This is a much more cumbersome form of wording and it takes the reader a longer time to work out what is being said.

It is the active voice you should be striving for in scientific literature, it is the best way to communicate your message to the reader. Unfortunately there is a feeling that papers should be written in the passive voice – where this has come from who knows but it seems to have been passed down from generation to generation.

It may stem from the perceived need for a certain languid detached style of the 'gentleman researcher' popular in previous centuries. This reflects modern mainstream writing at the time – look at the work of Charles Dickens or William Faulkner for long sentences with numerous clauses. The modern ear is less attuned to this style and we prefer short single preposition sentences (and this trend will continue with more and more being read online). Of all places where this is vital, scientific writing is the main one (note what a poor sentence **that** was – you didn't know what I was going to say until the end of it).

So make a conscious effort to write in the active voice avoiding long rolling sentences full of technical words. Remember you are trying to communicate, not show off.

5.7   Readability indices

You may be surprised to know that how easy it is to read a piece of writing can be measured. There are a number of readability indices and they can be very useful. They can allow you to pitch your language at an appropriate level for your intended audience. If you are interested in knowing more about these have a look at this article from the *British Medical Journal*:

http://www.ncbi.nlm.nih.gov/pmc/articles/PMC139036/pdf/1451.pdf

For those of you who don't want to go into such depths, how can you measure the readability of your paper? Well it's easier than you think. *Microsoft Word* actually has the facility of the *Flesch Reading Ease Index* and the *Flesch-Kincaid Grade Level*.

If you go to Tools   ➜   Options   ➜   Spelling and Auto-correction Proofing   ➜   **Check grammar with spelling** check box   ☐   This will bring the Show readability statistics check box to life. Tick it and from then on when you check grammar and spelling you will also get the readability score.

Try it, it's an informative exercise. I use it on everything I write and would recommend you do as well. And yes I have done it with this book – it has 18% passive sentences, a Flesch Reading ease of 60 and a Flesch-Kincaid Grade Level of 9.7 (i.e. someone in the Ninth Grade should be able to read this book).

5.8   Flow

The 'flow' of a paper is harder to define. It is the sum of the grammar, layout, readability, logic of argument and use of simple clear concepts. When reading fiction the flow is obvious – or perhaps I should say not obvious because it is so easy to read you almost forget you are reading.

This is not possible or necessary in a scientific paper but it is important that your reader can understand what you are trying to say. Again, make sure the grammar is good, make sure the readability indices are appropriate and most of all try to avoid showing off. The paper's important conclusions should be logically reached from the results.

It is actually very difficult to get a paper to flow properly and authors are not good judges of this. Get a colleague who does not know the field all that well to read it and comment. Even better, get someone who is not a scientist to read the paper – if they find it reads well (they do not have to understand all the language or concepts) then you are ready. If they do not, then make sure it is the technical parts they struggle with rather than the writing itself.

To repeat myself again, you are not writing *The Great Gatsby*, but you have a duty to the reader to try to make your paper as accessible as possible. Your reward if you do? More plaudits and probably more citations for your paper.

5.9   Layout

There isn't a great deal of flexibility with the look of your final published paper, which is more related to the journal in which it is published. However, when you submit your paper to peer review you can format it in a way that is easier on the eye. Submitting a close-typed tiny font size paper will immediately get the peer reviewer annoyed.

Use a standard font e.g. Times New Roman, Arial, Courier. Fancy fonts look odd in a scientific paper. Use a font size 11 or 12 that is easy to read. Avoid strange ink colors or lots of italics.

Make the different section headings obvious by putting them in a bigger font or in bold. Similarly make the sub-headings clear – don't have too many or the paper looks awkward to the reader.

Being visual animals, humans respond better to images – especially familiar ones, so make your paper looks like a paper (as well as sounding like one). Look at other papers in that journal and see how they are set out.

5.10   Abbreviations

Take care with abbreviations as not all your readers may be familiar with the ones you use. Always write an abbreviation in full the first time you use it and follow it with the recognized abbreviation in brackets after it.

Don't start making up your own abbreviations and don't use abbreviations in your title.

5.11   Units of Measurement

Measurements of length, height, weight, and volume should be reported in metric units (meter, kilogram, or liter); temperatures should be in degrees Celsius. Blood pressures should be in millimeters of mercury, unless other units are specifically required by the journal.

Journals vary in the units they use for reporting hematology, clinical chemistry, and other measurements, so make sure you check the Information for Authors of the particular journal. You should report laboratory information in both local and International System of Units (SI). Drug concentrations may be reported in either SI or mass units, but the alternative should be provided in parentheses where appropriate.

5.12   Line numbering

Finally, many reviewers like you to number the lines of text - this makes it easier for them when they are reviewing. They can say 'on line 21…..' instead of having to count the lines themselves. This can be done automatically in *Word* by going into *Page Layout* where you will see the *Line Numbers* option, clicking this automatically numbers the lines. Some journals don't like this being done so make sure there are no explicit instructions about this. If there aren't then do it – it looks professional and you want to remove as many reasons as possible for the peer reviewer to reject your paper.

5.13   Word Count

The maximum word count is not a rough guide - it is a rule. Before the days of electronic submission, you might have got away with a word count over the limit but nowadays these things are detected very quickly.

There are good reasons for limited sizes to papers – readers will only take in so much. In addition, most print journals have a limit to their physical size and associated print costs. Purely electronic journals are much less restricted in the size of the papers they can publish, but again think of the poor reader with many other competing articles to read. If you really have so much to say then consider splitting your pieces (not too much though - see 'Salami slicing' in Section 6.4) or perhaps writing a book instead!

Many journals want the word count written on the title page and/or during the submission process. Modern word processing programs do this easily enough (see under **Tools** in *Word*) but ensure you are counting the right words. The journal may specify word counts with or without title pages, abstracts or references, and if you count these you are wasting words you could have used more usefully.

5.14   Structure of your paper

The structure of a scientific paper is fairly uniform across disciplines and journals. It has evolved into a format that is logical and accepted by researchers.

As I discussed before it is essentially why we did something, how we did it and what we found. In terms that are more scientific this is represented as:

Introduction/background – this explains why the research was done, including what others have done before.

Method – how the research was performed.

Results – what was found.

Discussion – what the results mean, flaws in the study, implications.

Finally, this structure does not hold for all types of papers, just the research-based ones. Reviews, case reports, editorials have their own structure – which often varies from journal to journal. Generally editorials are plain text, but review papers may need particular sections – e.g. how the evidence was searched for, or implications of review findings or a plain language summary for patients. Journals often have a particular format for case reports so again **check first**.

5.15   The Title page

This may contain a number of different elements. Journals are specific in what they want so check. Generally speaking, it is a combination of:

- *The Title* – It goes without saying that the title is important. Generally, it is self-evident, describing the study or article content. You are not writing for a newspaper, but if you are doing a review article or a piece for a non-peer reviewed journal it is more acceptable to use a snappier title that might attract a reader. Some journals have rules about the title – for example if your paper is presenting a Randomized Controlled Trial then this should be in the title.

- *Subtitle* – sometimes there is an opportunity for a more descriptive subtitle. Use this facility by all means, but again this is not a newspaper, it is a document of scientific record, so be precise.

- *Keywords* – many journals ask for a list of keywords (check the maximum number they want) to allow readers to search for relevant papers. It is not difficult to do this of course, but it is difficult to do well. Take time with the keywords, this is how many people will search for and find your paper. The more specific you are the more likely they will be to find it. I would strongly advise you to look at *The National Library of Medicines* Medical Subject Headings (commonly called **MeSH**). These are the words that are used when identifying and indexing the articles in *PubMed* and by using them you are more likely to be in tune with those searching the databases. For more about MeSH and the terms it uses look here:

http://www.nlm.nih.gov/pubs/factsheets/mesh.html

- *Authors* – see Section 5.2 for a description and definition of authorship. The order of the authors has some significance – and can lead to conflict. The convention is that the first author listed is the main person who has conducted the study and written the paper. Sometimes two people fulfill this role and it is possible to have joint first authors. The last named author is generally the more senior person who usually has overseen the work. The remaining order can be discussed (hopefully without drawing blood!). There also needs to be a corresponding author who the reader or editor can contact with any queries about the paper. The corresponding author can be marked with an * and obviously their contact details need to be clear. Use surnames first with initials second (unless otherwise instructed by the journal). See below for an example of a layout.

- *Affiliations* – All authors' institutions, addresses and emails should be on the title page, usually denoted by numerical superscripts. The corresponding author should have all their contact details. An example is below:

Smith AB[1], Jones DC[2], Wilson EF[1], Presley EA[1].*

1. Institute of readable papers, Memphis.

2. Institute of grammar, Los Angeles.

Corresponding author – Dr DC Jones, Institute of grammer, University of Education, California, NT6. Tel 03429192020. Email: jonesword@ unied.ca.ac

- Some journals want the *copyright and conflict of interest statements* on the title page – check with the journal instructions page. If it is not specified then put the statement there. It is always good practice to add these statements whether asked for or not. Here is some guidance to help you construct one of your own if you need to:

http://content.nejm.org/cgi/content/full/361/19/1896

5.16 Abstract

The abstract of your paper is extremely important – it may well be the only part of your paper that most people read. Actually, the *conclusion* to your abstract is the only part of your paper most people will read!

Journal Indexers like *PubMed* provide access to the abstract to allow readers to decide if they want to get hold of the whole paper. So think of your abstract as an advertisement for your paper, containing its message but in a very concise form.

It may also be the only thing that the editor reads before deciding to send it for peer review or reject immediately:

http://www.ncbi.nlm.nih.gov/pmc/articles/PMC515189/

It is obvious from the above that it is well worth spending time getting your abstract right. Many people write the paper and then put together a quick abstract just before they submit it. This is a mistake. A good abstract is hard to write because it has a strict word count but needs to convey the essential nature of your study.

Think of it like a blurb for a book – you want someone to read your paper and the abstract for it is the gateway to your work. The reader may be attracted by an interest in your findings or your paper might contain a particular piece of data they are looking for. The good abstract conveys accuracy but with brevity – a difficult combination to achieve indeed. An abstract almost has too much power – a busy professional does not have time to scour all potential papers so we rely heavily on the abstract.

Have I hammered this point home enough times now? Take time with the abstract. It will, to repeat myself, be read many more times than your complete paper.

The general structure of the abstract for scientific papers is pretty standard with an *Introduction/Background* (or sometimes rationale for the study), *Methods and/or materials* (this may be broken into sections such as type or study or participants), *Results/Findings*, *Conclusions/Implications*. There are numerous small variations used in different journals so that more information is included. Some have a section for study design, some for implications of research, others want a background section. Essentially these are simply subdivisions of the standard abstract criteria.

Make sure you check with the journal you are submitting to and conform to exactly the abstract format they want. It will only cause annoyance if you get such a simple thing wrong.

Some other types of article, rather than using a structured abstract, have a summary of a few hundred words at the beginning. This might be your big chance to hook the reader, so again, spend time getting it right.

5.17   The Introduction

As discussed previously, a scientific paper is a device for communication. Human beings communicate best using narrative structures, and a paper is no different. The introduction therefore is the scene setter for your paper. It introduces the 'characters' and gives some background as to where they came from and how they got there. It indicates why the study was undertaken and what questions are being asked.

Writing the introduction can be tricky. It shouldn't be too long or the reader will lose interest before they have even started. Most papers are looking at one aspect, or small range of aspects, of a disease or treatment. The exception to this is population-based studies but often they are split into a number of smaller papers. So in any paper type there is no need for the introduction to be particularly long.

Avoid details that are better placed in other sections. There is a tendency to do a literature review in the introduction as a way of making the study rationale stronger. Don't do this. A review of literature is better in the discussion section. Similarly aspects of the methods (e.g. why you chose one method above another) are better put in the methods or discussion sections.

5.18   Methods

It goes without saying that the Methods section has to be accurate. This is where those with the real knowledge will judge your paper. If you have devised a new method or your results are unexpected, others will want to repeat your experiment to test your results. If they can't follow what you have done or can't replicate it you are going to look foolish (at best). So be precise, clear and comprehensive when you write your methods section.

I use the term experiment in its widest sense. It doesn't matter if you are doing the most basic of molecular research or presenting a series of clinical cases, the reader needs to know how you did it. What conditions did you use, what was your case definition, could your experiment have been contaminated in some way?

For complex study protocols, it might be too much to detail these in the paper. Many journals now allow extra files to be uploaded to the electronic version of their journal. This is not a reason though for skimping on important detail in your paper.

If you have your own or a departmental website you could also put more detail on it – with a link from the paper. A warning though if you do this: if your paper is in a journal such as *PubMed* for perpetuity then make sure your web-link is also maintained.

5.19 Statistics

Nothing brings greater consternation to most authors of papers – and readers – than the stats. Paradoxically though most authors make their stats as complicated as possible. I think this is a way of showing how clever they are but usually it confuses the reader. There might of course be another reason for using complex stats – to try to hide the deficiencies of the method or to try to rescue something out of the results.

Statistics in a research study are used for a number of reasons:

1. Prior to the study to make sure enough numbers will be recruited to demonstrate real effect of an intervention (a power calculation)

2. To allow analysis of the findings of a study. To measure the size and direction of a result and to look for possible biases

and confounders in the results that might cast doubt on them.

3. To compare different studies in a rigorous way.

4. To allow representation of the data in a form that is more readily understandable to the reader.

This final point is the most important use of statistics. Readers don't want to trail through columns of data – they want a mean or median. They don't want to have to work out if your sample size was large enough for statistical significance – they want a 'p' value. They don't want to have to calculate the real clinical impact of your findings – they want an odds ratio or a relative risk or an absolute risk.

Each of these is a numerical representation of the data and allows us to quickly assess the importance of the findings. As most journal readers only have a limited understanding of stats then stick to the parameters they understand. Everyone understands simple descriptive stats – percentages, means etc., so give these. Add 'p- value' and significance levels also – most readers will still be with you. If you are going to use complex stats then use this rule of thumb:

- Be sure yourself that you should be using them
- Explain to the reader why you are doing this
- Don't do the calculations yourself

I personally would go as far as to say that, unless you are fully conversant with complex stats, you shouldn't do any calculations yourself. This of course doesn't include the simple descriptive stats of means, medians etc. Don't find a free stats program on the web, put your data into it and see what comes out. If you do then you are proof of the phrase 'lies, damn lies and statistics'.

This brings us neatly to...

5.20 Statisticians

As we all know statisticians are very clever people. It is good to have very clever people associated with your paper. It is also good to get statisticians to take all the numbers and convert them into an 'answer' for you.

But be careful.

I would have no doubt that you should get advice from a statistician about all but the simplest study. They will be an invaluable companion through the rocky slopes of study design and results analysis. They will stop you making random calculations in complex statistical programs and looking a fool when the paper is published.

But remember that your readers are not statisticians so keep it as simple as you can. If you end up with various Greek letters all over your paper then you run the risk of readers being suspicious that you are trying to hide something! To repeat, statistics are merely representations of your data. Make sure they represent to the reader of your paper what you should represent and what you want to represent.

Finally, add the statistician as an author of your paper (as long as they fulfill the authorship criteria for that journal). Not only is it the right thing to do, it makes it obvious to the reader that you had statistical support. It is also useful if someone queries the stats in the paper then you can pass the query straight on to the statistician!

5.21 Ethics and Trial Numbers

It is increasingly (and rightly so) important to make sure you obtain ethical approval for your work. This should be clearly written in the methods section of your paper and should include:

- The statement that ethical approval was obtained for the study.

- The Ethical committee/Institutional Review Board that gave this approval.

- An Ethics number if you received one.

Additionally if you have conducted experiments on animals, most countries only allow this if the laboratory has been licensed. Put the details of this license in your paper.

Some research institutions also have a Research Board which oversees the research being done in that institution. This can be separate from the Ethics Committee or combined, but usually deals with the applicability of the research, its funding and its conduct in relation to the institution rather than the wider world. This does of course have overlaps with the Ethics Committee. Some institutions do not have these boards but if yours does then state this approval in the paper.

If you are submitting a controlled clinical trial to a journal it is increasingly common to be asked for a trial number. This is given by a Clinical Trials Register and you will need to apply for this to the appropriate register. All clinical trials should be registered – not only does this allow a certain amount of standardization, it means that trials can be located quickly and comprehensively by fellow researchers (see publication bias in Section 3.7).

All reputable journals will now ask for you to insert your trial number when you submit your paper:

http://www.icmje.org/recommendations/browse/publishing-and-editorial-issues/clinical-trial-registration.html

Save yourself time and apply for a trial number as soon as the trial is set-up. Waiting to have a number assigned retrospectively will delay submission of your paper.

5.22 Results

Now we are getting to the nitty gritty of the paper and you can begin to show the world what you are made of.

The results section is so named as it is the place where you write your results. It is not a place where you discuss your findings or their implications – this is for the next section.

Sometimes it is necessary to put some explanation of how you did something – especially if it was unexpected or caused deviation from your intended method. This should be examined at length in the discussion but it may be necessary to also mention it in the results section to clarify particular steps.

The results are presented in text, numbers and diagrams. Writing a good results section requires a balance between words, numbers and diagrams. Tables are useful as they convey a lot of information concisely. Don't repeat all the data in the text if it is in the table – it is advisable though to mention any unexpected results or to draw the reader's attention to particularly important findings rather than assuming the reader has spotted them in the table.

It is usually obvious what type of format the results are best illustrated with – graphs, pictures of patients or lab results or investigation results e.g. X-rays, tables, plots, histology. Think carefully about what will aid the reader and what will distract.

Important results MUST be in the paper, but if there is more data then consider, as with methods, whether it is worth posting separately on the web. A mass of data or densely packed tables will be off-putting for the reader.

The balance between too much information and not enough is difficult. It depends on the type of paper you are writing and the journal type. But always try to keep the reader in mind.

Don't hide away inconvenient results – these happen and are best discussed openly. Those who hide results are doing a disservice to science and to themselves. Science thrives on debate and disagreement so show your results and defend them if you want to. Concealing results can distort your whole specialty and could have serious consequences if you are found out.

Make sure all tables, graphs etc. are clearly labeled with what they show. Make sure they are referred to in the text so the reader knows to make the link. Don't have orphans that the reader can't place in the text.

For more about images and publication see Section 5.29.

5.23 Discussion

This is the bit you have been waiting to write. It gives you the opportunity to tie everything together and to discuss the implications of what you have found. This is your time in the spotlight!

Needless to say the discussion has to be written clearly and precisely. If it is too long it won't be read properly. Too short and you will miss important detail. Extraneous words need to be rigorously weeded out – which means rewrite, rewrite, rewrite.

Keep your sentences short and make a single point in each. Make sure each point you make follows logically one after another. Keep to the active voice rather than the passive (see Section 5.6)

Here are some tips to help:

1. Start the discussion with a summary of the literature surrounding your work. This is not a review piece though – the paper is about your work not someone else's, so keep it brief. You are trying to give a wider context for your work not rewrite others' papers.

2. Follow this by discussing how your results compare with the findings of others. Are they the same? Are they different? If so, why was your method different? (better? biased?). Have you shown up flaws or inconsistencies in others' work?

3. What are the implications of your work? Have they confirmed someone else's findings? Have they shown a new way of doing a technique.? Will your findings have an impact upon patient care?

4. Are your findings generalizable? This means you might have performed a perfect study and analyzed it fully but it only works in your patient group.

5. All papers must (but rarely do) discuss potential biases and flaws. Many authors shy away from this in case they undermine their own paper. But **all** studies and papers have flaws. It is far better to discuss these openly and to refute them or explain that they were unavoidable than to ignore them. Honesty is vital in science but it also disarms the hostile reader.

6. Suggestions for further work – in its highest sense research is not about individuals but about the combined work of a number of researchers. It really is 'standing on the shoulders of giants' as we take someone else's work and use it to

look deeper into a particular area. This 'chain' of research is mirrored in the paper – you start by describing where others got to and finish by suggesting where the next steps after your own work should be. Always include this in your discussion – what should be done next? How should it be done in the light of your own findings? Think of yourself passing the baton on to the next person – research is like an ant colony all working hard for the common good.

Sometimes journals ask for a conclusion as well at the end of the discussion section. This is effectively a short summary of the main findings.

All the rest

Now you have finished your paper you are very keen to get it sent off (and resume normal life without its gray shadow hanging over your head). But you are not finished yet! There are still a number of things to think about and add. You are bound to forget one of these so here is a list to remind you:

1.   References

These are probably the biggest irritation once the paper is finished. I usually suggest that you deal with them as you write but I can't say I do this myself. I find it better just to get the words on the page and then tidy up later – which does make referencing much harder.

Some tips for references:

- Check the style preferred by the journal – the two alternatives are the Vancouver style and the Harvard style. The Harvard style uses the author's name and date of publication in the body of the text, and the bibliography is given alphabetically by author. The Vancouver system uses a number series to indicate references which are listed in numerical order as they appear in the text. There are some variations on these two systems so make sure you check which system is used and whether any variations are required. This will be clearly stated in the instructions for authors so check before you write the paper – and certainly before you submit it.

Here is an excellent summary of the different reference styles with examples and details of some variations:

http://bma.org.uk/about-the-bma/bma-library/ask-for-help/reference-styles

- Unless instructed otherwise put the references in the text in square brackets   [   ]. They will probably end up as superscript but if you do this yourself it can give problems with formatting.

- If you use *Endnote* take care as some electronic submission systems can't deal with this conversion. Although very useful I don't use *Endnote* for this reason.

- Keep your references pertinent and minimal. Don't try to show off by inserting as many references as you can. If you are referencing background information then choose either a review or a seminal paper rather than six references on the same topic.

- Conversely you must reference all statements you make – unless you are stating something novel or you do not have evidence (which you should state). References are ways of linking your work to the general corpus of research and to allow others to see what your work is based on.

- If you are going to reference only your own work then make sure you are justified in doing so.

- Information from manuscripts not yet in press can either have this appended to the reference or be placed directly in the text (preferable). Similarly for data solely reported at meetings, or personal communications, cite only in the text, not as formal references.

- References to books or book chapter references – these should give the authors' names (or authors of the appropriate chapter), the name of the book, the name of the chapter if appropriate, the editor(s), publisher, place of publication and year.

- Web references take a different format and you should check with the journal you are submitting to. There are no standard rules for citing web references – some journals are happy with a simple link, others a more complicated format that includes the date last accessed. Marking web references in the text also differs between journals – some keep the same format as non-web references, others use a 'w' before the reference number to indicate that it is a web reference.

  Once again make sure you check with the journal which format they prefer.

5.25 Drug names

Generally use the generic (non-proprietary) name of the drug. If the proprietary name is to be used then place it in brackets after the generic name and add the manufacturer.

5.26 Gene names

Use gene names approved by the Human Gene Organisation the first time the gene is mentioned in the paper. For gene sequences give the accession number in the methods section.

5.27   Web extras

As mentioned previously, some print journals give the option of putting part of the paper on the web. This is to save print space and can be used for long lists of references, detailed descriptions of methods or more in depth statistical analysis. The journal will probably contact you if it wants to do this.

Some journals also offer the options of further illustrations of your work on their website. This may be illustrations or videos or even podcasts of your work. Think about these when you are writing the paper and if you have the option they can be a good way of generating extra interest.

5.28   Consent

If it is in any way possible to identify a patient from a description or illustration in the paper then you need the patient's consent for this. This should be written consent and this should be indicated somewhere in the paper – usually under the picture itself.

Different journals have different policies on when they need consent so make sure you check this early in case you lose contact with the patient. Here are a couple of links to examples of journal policy and specimen consent forms:

One from the New England Journal Medicine: http://authors.nejm.org/help/patientid.pdf

And one from the British Medical Journal:

http://resources.bmj.com/bmj/authors/editorial-policies/copy_of_patient-confidentiality

5.29   Images

Many print journals will ask you to pay for any images you have in your paper. If there are a lot of images this can get expensive, so check the journals policy before you submit.

Electronic journals do not charge for images and can of course offer almost unlimited space for them. Many authors baulk at the thought of paying for publication with an open access journal but sometimes the costs are equivalent when images are considered.

Make sure anything non-text such as images, tables, diagrams are clearly labeled and mentioned in the text. Having an illustration that can't be placed by the reader in the paper doesn't make you any friends.

Again, don't forget, images may allow patient identification so get consent and record this.

Images must be of an acceptable quality or the journal might not accept them. For a very useful guide to the formatting of images and tables have a look at this link:

http://www.icmje.org/recommendations/browse/manuscript-preparation/

5.30   Conflicts of interest

Many journals now specifically ask about this and ask you to add a statement to your paper. If the journal you are submitting to doesn't ask this, it is still a good idea to add a statement. It looks professional and suggests to the editor and reviewers that you know what you are doing. And it is good practice anyway – whatever type of communication you are involved with, it is important that your audience knows where you might be coming from. Without doubt it is better to declare a potential conflict of interest rather than having it come to light later. This looks suspicious even when it is not.

You can copy the format of some of the statements described in Section 5.15 if you need to make one and the journal does not provide a template.

5.31   Authorship Criteria

Again some journals specifically ask for a statement on this when you submit the paper. Even if they don't it is good practice to describe each author's contribution (See section 5.2).

5.32   Acknowledgments

For those who have helped with the study or paper it is appropriate to acknowledge them in the paper. Those who fail the authorship criteria can be mentioned here.

Usually acknowledgements are at the end of the manuscript – before the references. For more information of who and what to acknowledge have a look at this link to the ICJME site:

http://www.icmje.org/recommendations/browse/roles-and-responsibilities/defining-the-role-of-authors-and-contributors.html

Section 6. Submitting your paper

Ok so your research is done, your paper written whilst your friends go for a coffee without you, it's now time to submit. Not difficult of course but remember the number one rule of getting published - **attention to detail.**

Make sure you know how the journal likes submissions – is it electronic or paper? Do you submit and upload via the website? Check the format the journal wants your paper in – do they accept all versions of *Word*? Is it ok to use the Mac word processing program, *Pages*? Single spaced or double spaced? Do they want the abstract in the paper? Do they want you to take your names off the paper so that the reviewers can be masked? Should you avoid *Endnote* – as some file conversions struggle if this is used?

The list is almost endless but it will all be clear in the instructions for authors what formatting and presentation they want. It's worth being obsessive about this and double checking you have adhered to what they want. As you will start seeing only what you want to see after three or four rewrites get someone else to check it.

One thing that is worth thinking about, unless the journal specifically asks you not to, is numbering each line on the paper. Some journals prefer you to do this. It makes the reviewer's job easier, as they can refer to specific places in the text more easily. I would suggest doing this for all papers as making the reviewer's job easier is not a bad idea. To actually do it is not as fearsomely difficult as it sounds – *Word* will do it for you:

On the **File** menu, click **Page Setup**, and then click the **Layout** tab. In the **Apply to** box, click **Whole document**. Click **Line Numbers**. Select the **Add line numbering** check box, and then select the options you want.

6.1   Covering letter to the editor

Most journals require a covering letter to the editor. This is usually something that states that the work is original, has not been submitted to another journal and that all the authors agree to publication.

Some journals have a set format for these letters whilst others use a tick box system on their electronic submission site.

Even if a covering letter is not required by the journal most authors prefer to add one. There is nothing wrong with this but it shouldn't be used as a place to 'sell' the paper i.e. tell the editor why it is a great paper and why it should be published. Most editors don't read these covering letters anyway and if they do will make a decision based on other factors. There is certainly nothing wrong with putting an argument for your paper but I think generally it is wasted effort.

What is sometimes worth doing is to mention that the results of the paper were also presented at a meeting (see next section). This is especially so if the meeting is linked to the journal – a number of Academic Societies have scientific meetings and require that subsequent papers be submitted to their house journal. If you mention this in the covering letter this could help with the editor's judgment of your paper.

If there is no specified format for the covering letter I would ensure that the following contents are included:

1. The title of the paper.

2. Confirming it is being submitted to that named journal. If you subsequently have to submit to another journal remember to change this – you would be surprised how many people don't!

3. State that the paper is not being submitted to any other journal.

4. State that all authors agree to the submission and publication of the paper.

5. Conflicts of interest or financial associations should be in the paper itself, but you can add these to the covering letter stating that they are in the paper.

6. Sign and date the letter. If it is a paper submission get the other authors to sign. If not then the corresponding author should state they are signing on behalf of all the authors.

6.2   Presenting the results (meetings etc.)

It is common for the results of a study to be presented at scientific meetings before being submitted for publication. Meetings allow findings to be disseminated much more rapidly than do papers.

Authors sometimes worry about whether they are guilty of dual publication (see next section) or that their paper will be less likely to be accepted because the results are already out. This isn't a great problem in reality – in fact if your presentation/poster has created a stir then the editor might be keener to accept the paper.

Some meetings are arranged by scientific societies who also have journals. Having a presentation at a meeting may mean you are obliged to submit to their house journal. This could be good or bad of course.

If you have submitted a paper to a journal and the results are likely to be picked up by the press then the journal may not want you to go public with your results until they have published the paper. You will need to liaise with the journal if this happens.

6.3   Linked publications

If your paper is a subsequent paper in a series and the others have been published in that journal then make this clear. Some journals ask you during submission if there are any linked publications but most don't. Make it clear in your covering letter to the editor or to the editorial staff that this paper is related to the other papers published.

6.4   Fraud

There are a large number of methods of committing research fraud – and with the rise of the internet the number is on the increase. Fraud can occur anywhere from the study plan, to the research itself, to the stats, interpreting the results and hiding the negative results. Whole books are written on this topic and they are beyond the scope of this book.

How serious you perceive fraud I guess depends on a number of things, but it is taken very seriously by journals. There have been examples of practitioners having their license to practice revoked after being found guilty of research fraud.

There are four particular types of misdeeds associated with paper writing and submission (as opposed to "making the results up" types of fraud) which you might be tempted to commit but shouldn't:

1. **Dual submission** – the lengthy process that can be involved in submitting, reviewing and publishing a paper can be frustrating. Even more so if you have the paper rejected and you have to start the process again. It is therefore tempting to submit to more than one journal at once to save time. This is a big no-no for editors. For them it means using resources – including peer reviewers (who are a surprisingly scarce resource) for a paper that might be withdrawn. It's tempting I know to dual submit but remember that editors talk to each other and many will take a very dim view if they catch you – including contacting your employer as has happened in some cases. If swift publication is important, look for a journal with a very short decision/publication time – many post these on their websites.

2. **Salami slicing** – this is the term sometimes given to a series of papers arising from one study where each paper describes a small aspect of the study. This means the authors get multiple papers from one study. It is perhaps not fair to describe this as fraud – certainly large studies would be expected to publish a series of papers. If however you have a single small study and produce a series of papers that are essentially very similar this is effectively (self) plagiarism, which is fraud. The best protection from this is to be honest with yourself (does this study REALLY justify two or more papers?) and to reference your other paper so that the reviewers do not feel you are trying to conceal something.

3. **Plagiarism/non-referencing** – This is perhaps one of the commonest forms of research fraud. Certainly in writing the paper it becomes tempting to cut and paste other people's words into your paper. Don't do this – it is, at the very least, embarrassing when you are found out (remember that the referees are from the same field and so are the authors of the paper you have sampled, so there is a good chance they will

see your paper). Plagiarism can also be accidental – you may need to quote parts of others' papers to make your point. To avoid plagiarism firstly and most obviously, write in your own words. Secondly, if you do need to quote extensively from others' papers then make sure you reference **fully**.

One last point about plagiarism (and this blends with the 'salami slicing' discussed above), essentially you CAN self-plagiarize if you use results, large chunks of texts or illustrations without referencing other works. That fits the definition of plagiarism. Presenting at meetings or in personal communications is fine though.

4. **Unjustified authorship** – we discussed in Section 5.2 what authorship means and how to define it. That this is an issue is illustrated by the need for journals to define it. It is of course long established practice for a Head of Department to have their name on a paper – even if they did not materially contribute to the paper. This is less acceptable nowadays though of course difficult to prove. Some journals require a statement confirming authorship and rightly so – it is a privilege to be a published author, with the benefits this can bring, so it is not right that someone gets this because of their position or because they have some power (e.g. career progression) over the real authors.

These seem relatively minor when you compare them with some of the more serious frauds, such as entire experiments being fraudulently conducted or reported. But in their own way they are important – both for your own scientific integrity and the fact they skew the database of original publications. More pragmatically, if you get caught the editor will be very angry - disproportionately so you might feel. Editors take their jobs very seriously – they are upholding the standards of their journals and of scientific research. A single piece of fraud both undermines this principle and casts doubt on your entire work. Without doubt the paper will be rejected and the editor may contact your employing institution to let them know what you did.

To read a fascinating example of the potential consequences of research fraud have a look at this from the British Medical Journal (you will have to register to see the full article, but it is free to do so):

http://www.bmj.com/cgi/content/extract/331/7511/281

If you have any questions about research and publication misconduct, or simply want to voyeuristically enjoy what messes other have got themselves into, have a look at the Committee on Publications ethics (COPE) website:

http://publicationethics.org/

This is a truly excellent organization that works to counter research/publication fraud and to create guidelines in areas where things aren't so clear.

6.5   The review process

Until the rise of online paper submission, an author would finish their paper, attach a covering letter and send to the editor of the journal. Usually they would receive an acknowledgement slip and they would then wait for some weeks (or months) for the peer reviewers to assess their paper and get back to the editor who would write with a decision.

Nowadays most journals use online submission. You are automatically told how the paper is progressing at various stages. Generally you will notice it is the peer review stage that is the rate limiting step. Peer reviewers are providing this service free of charge and in their own time so it is difficult for editorial staff to pressurize them too much.

Most journals now ask peer reviewers to agree to submit their reviews within a specific time limit. If the reviewers exceed this there is little that can be done. After a longer period a new reviewer may need to be found - which itself takes time.

Generally it is not worth hassling the editorial staff about what is happening to your paper. If the paper has got 'stuck' at a particular part of the submission process it is worth emailing them to make sure it has been uploaded correctly. Only if the reviewers are taking an inordinate amount of time is it worth sending a gentle query about when you might receive a decision. But again there isn't much they can do except perhaps to give the reviewer a gentle nudge.

In my experience editorial staff are unfailingly helpful but usually busy – answering queries like yours.

If it is essential for you to have your paper published quickly then you may be able to check on the journal's website for the average turnaround time for a paper. Some can do it within 2 weeks with obliging peer reviewers.

6.6   Response to reviewers

Once the editor has the reports from the reviewer they will make a decision on your paper. This decision will be heavily influenced by the peer reviews, but there are other factors e.g. current paper backload, print space, similar papers about to be published, which have an influence in the decision.

What is certain is that if the peer reviews (generally there are at least two peer reviews) are all poor, your paper will not be accepted.

If one review is good and the other bad then the decision might depend on a third reviewer but again it depends on the journal policy and current backlog of papers.

Though different journals have different ways of conveying their decisions there are only a limited number of responses they can give:

1. Accepted as is – this is rare as it means the paper (including grammar and layout) is perfect as is. Well done if this EVER happens to you.

2. Accepted after changes based on satisfactory response to the reviewers' comments - this means the paper is accepted as long as you make the suggested changes (see the next section for more about this).

3. Rejected – apart from its obvious meaning this also means that the journal relinquishes any hold on your paper and you are free to submit elsewhere.

4. Alternative formats – some journals will reject your paper but suggest you submit it as a short communication or letter to the editor. It's up to you what you do with this. It essentially means that your work is accepted – as long as you convert to the desired format. If you are not happy with that and do want a full paper published then communicate this so you can submit to an alternative journal.

5. Alternative journal – some journals, which are part of a larger suite of journals, may suggest, if your paper is rejected, that you submit to an appropriate journal of the same group. Again it depends what you want from your paper whether you decide to do this.

6.7 Resubmission

If the decision was 'accepted after revisions', this means you need to alter the paper as per the reviewers' and editor's comments. The way to do this is to deal with the comments one by one and list them in a separate document. This is then sent to the editor with the revised paper – name this document 'response to reviewers'.

Whilst it is very important to deal with all the reviewers' comments that doesn't mean you have to **agree** with all their comments. If you do disagree then state that in your response document, giving the reasons why you don't think these changes should be made. Reviewers are not infallible and it is the editor's call as to which points are essential for change.

When you submit your response to reviewers DON'T be angry or sarcastic. Answer each point (even if it seems insulting to you) in a professional manner. Failure to do so will irritate the editor and make him or her wonder if they want an author like you in their journal.

If your resubmission requires a change of format – and almost invariably it is a shortening of the paper - then make sure you know the restrictions of that format in that journal. If you don't do this the paper will be returned to you for modification, so save yourself some time and get it right first time.

6.8 What to do if you are rejected

If your paper is rejected completely it is generally not worth trying to argue the point. Some journals have a formal appeal system that you can invoke if you feel strongly that a wrong decision has been made.

Either using this system or, if there isn't a system – in which case you should write to the editor directly – and you feel strongly enough to appeal, here are a few tips:

1. Be polite and don't get annoyed with the editor or reviewers, it will make things worse.

2. If you feel you have grounds for appeal then be specific – there is no point saying 'don't you realize that this is a great paper?'. The commonest reason for appeal is that the author feels the reviewers have misjudged the paper in some way or that the reviewers are biased. Of course this can happen – reviewers are often working in the same field as you and either don't like you (yes really some people don't like YOU) or want to hinder your work so they can get theirs out. This is actually very rare – although the paranoia that this is happening is very common. If you do feel this has happened then you need to let the editor know - although you better have good evidence.

3. If your appeal is successful the editor may send the paper for a further review (often an editorial board member). Their decision is likely to be final.

4. If the editor rejects your review out of hand then it is best to accept this – though there is no harm politely asking why.

6.9   Submitting to another journal

Although you are naturally disappointed by rejection you must concentrate on the positives:

• You now have experience of submitting a paper so you are already better at the game.

• Your paper has been gone through by at least two experts in your field, for free, and they have let you have their comments. So there is no excuse not to produce a better paper.

Have a think about the next journal you are going to submit to – it may be obvious in your field of work or you may have a bigger choice. Think if you need to drop down a 'level' to a lower ranking journal. Ask your co-authors and colleagues whether that is the right course. Get advice from those who are experienced with papers and see what journal they would suggest.

When you submit to the next journal, there is no need to mention that the paper was rejected from another journal. Submit the paper as if it were the first submission, making sure you have removed the previous journal's name from the covering letter and that you have formatted as per the new journal's requirements. Once again, sloppiness will lead to a very fast return of the paper.

There is no reason why you shouldn't continue to submit to journals each time you are rejected. Hopefully you will have learnt a little from each one and your paper is continually improving. It's demoralizing and time consuming but Hey, I did warn you, didn't I?

If this is what is happening then you will have to go to some of the publications even lower down the pecking order – perhaps a non-peer reviewed journal or online publication.

I will repeat that the greatest attribute for getting a paper accepted is persistence. This doesn't mean unthinkingly sending off the same paper each time, but using the process – the reviewers' comments, the editor's words and the advice and support of your colleagues to improve your paper until it is accepted.

Will all this make you a better person? Probably not, but you will have learned something that Confucius knew thousands of years ago - it does not matter the number of times we fall but the number of times we rise when we fall.

Section 7. Ten ways to make sure your paper is rejected

Not surprisingly there are more ways of getting your paper rejected than there are of getting it accepted. However there are some really good ways of getting it rejected almost immediately.

In no particular order here are the Top 10 ways of achieving almost instantaneous rejection. Those marked with a * are the fast-track ways to get your paper rejected i.e. without even being deemed worthy of peer review!

1. Design and conduct a poor study.

2. Ignore the journal's instructions for authors and just write the paper.*

3. Write a paper that is full of grammatical and spelling errors.*

4. Insult a colleague or author of a similar work in your paper.

5. Make derogatory comments about the patient you are writing about.*

6. Keep the whole project to yourself jealously guarding the paper from others' comments or criticism.

7. Take personal offence at the reviewers' or editor's comments and unleash a torrent of abuse at the unfairness of it all.

8. Cut and paste large parts of other people's work into your paper and accidentally forget to reference it.

9. Insist your name is on a paper written by someone junior even though you have not been involved in the work. Compound this by not reading the paper prior to submission.

10. Submit the paper to two journals simultaneously and find that the same reviewers have been used.

Finally, good ways to ensure rejection AND embarrass yourself/co-authors/department:

1. Lose the memory stick with all the study patient names and clinical details on it. Compound this by also having identifiable images, not password protecting the memory stick, and losing the stick in a public place – perhaps near a newspaper office.

2. Presenting at a meeting that has an associated journal copyright and submit to a different journal without permission.

3. Lose a patient's consent form – you have submitted a really interesting case, taken some fantastic images, written a great paper but the journal wants proof of the patient's consent to having their image shown. You forgot to do this and the patient is now lost to follow-up.

4. Not having ethical approval and being asked for it by the journal. If the study has involved human or animal experiments then this could be more serious than just having the paper rejected.

5. Submit to an open access journal, go through the review process, address the reviewers' comments, resubmit the paper, have it accepted and then realize you can't pay the publication fee.

Section 8.   Resources for authors

There are some excellent resources for journal authors out there. Here follows some of those that I have found most useful – both for writing in general and writing specifically for scientific publications.

You should also look within your own areas of expertise, often there are articles describing how to publish within the particular constraints or formats of your own discipline. I would suggest doing a wide search for these perhaps using Google or Google Scholar.

Useful Websites

The International Committee of Medical Journal Editors' website is packed full of useful information on all aspects of publishing of papers:

http://www.icmje.org/index.html

Committee on Publication Ethics is an organization that provides advice and guidance on all aspects of academic publication. There are a number of cases on their website which are illuminating:

http://publicationethics.org/

For those in the UK there is a single application for ethical approval and it can be found here:

http://www.nres.nhs.uk/The Cochrane Collaboration and Cochrane library are a rich source of information about clinical research.

http://www.cochrane.org/

Useful Books

As mentioned the definitive book about the conventions and rules of writing is the classic *Elements of Style* by W. Strunk and E.B. White. It's a small book but contains all the rules you will ever need. You will be able to get this via Amazon or your local bookshop.

On Writing is by the author Stephen King and describes his approach to (fiction) writing. It is full of good advice and invaluable for any sort of writing.

The Trouble With Medical Journals is an excellent book by the ex-*British Medical Journal* editor Richard Smith. Drawing from his experience it discusses the strengths and weaknesses of modern academic journals.

It is often stated that a good writer needs to be a good reader and extending this if you want to write a good paper then you need to know how to read a paper. There is no better book to teach you this than *How to Read a Paper* by Trisha Greenhalgh.

If you have made it this far then you must be keen to be published. I hope this book will help you achieve your ambition. There is of course no magic formula for ensuring publication, but if you are honest (with yourself and others), interested in your subject, you write to be clear rather than to show off how clever you are, and most of all if you are persistent, then you will see your name in print.

Now, enough of reading how it should be done. Close this book, switch on your computer and start writing!